How to Create Wealth

RAE JONES

Copyright © 2011 Author Name

ISBN: 146372800X
ISBN-13: 978-1463728007

DEDICATION

This book is dedicated to my first job at 14.

To the man who believed in me when we were 10,000 miles from nowhere and I felt small scared and lost.

And to my parents.
Thank you.

CONTENTS

Dedication — i

1 Personal Wealth — Pg # 1

2 Budget — Pg # 6

3 Estimate Your Income — Pg # 10

4 Estimate Your Expenses — Pg #12

5 Balance Your Spending Plan — Pg #20

6 Adjust Your Budget — Pg #21

7 Long Term Planning — Pg #37

8 The Value of Time — Pg #41

About the Author — Pg # 45

1 PERSONAL WEALTH

Every where at every moment is an opportunity to make money. It's like pennies from heaven. Are you too good for pennies? That is the difference between those who are wealthy and those who are not.

"Beware of little expenses;
a small leak will sink a great ship"
~Benjamin Franklin

Here is some truth about wealth:
It happens when you pay close attention to your money.

It happens when you are intimate with your finances

Disciplined when it comes to budgeting

It happens when you are AWARE of where the money goes.

The point is, it takes time, effort, energy and attention on finances to create wealth. It is a lifestyle, it will be a change and it is an ADVENTURE!

Truth:
Unless you try something new, think about things differently and embark upon a risky undertaking with an uncertain outcome, you WILL NOT grow. You will not change, and quite possibly you will never achieve the wealth you deserve.

<u>Even More Truth.</u>
YOU DESERVE WEALTH!

"I've been rich, I've been poor. Rich is better."
~Sophie Tucker

Personal wealth is nothing more than applying a roadmap to monetary decisions plus time. It is a simple equation of:

$$(Obtain + Budget + Save + Spend) \times Time = Wealth.$$

Wealth happens or doesn't happen on based upon the four variables of obtain, budget, save and spend.

You don't have to be a millionaire to begin with, you just have to pay attention to what you DO HAVE and start from there.

It goes without saying that the key component of achieving personal wealth is PLANNING.

You wouldn't go hiking without a map, and you are not going to lose that extra 20 pounds without a change in your diet or exercise, then, what makes you think that you are going to wake up wealthy without changing something in your money habits?

THE key component of creating personal wealth is planning. This is a dynamic process that requires your time and attention, regular monitoring and reevaluation. There are five steps.

1.) **Assessment** - You must first get very intimate and HONEST with where you currently are. There is no right or wrong answer. You do not have to tell anyone else, this is for you and you alone. This is not a drill to make you feel guilty or a bad person.

You are a great person! You deserve to be wealthy and happy! This is the first step, and the first step is always the hardest. Do that NOW! Do not keep reading without honestly assessing your situation. Done? Good. Let's continue.

2.) **Setting Goals** - This is an easy step. I want you to dream! Set the bar high! There is nothing that you can't do, remember, time is on your side. Let your goals reflect your dreams. Set short term goals (1-3 years) and long term goals (15-20 years) Some examples are 'retire by 65 with $1 mil.', or 'pay off all credit cards within 3 years'. They are your goals, get creative, think outside the box, see how far your mind will take you.

"Shoot for the moon, even if you miss you will land among the stars." ~Brian Thomas Littrel

3.) **Create a Plan** - This is the budget part. The analytical, time consuming, truth hitting you right between the eyes of where your money is going part. But don't worry, I will walk you through the process and it will be easy. A step by step guide to creating a budget you can KEEP! Not one that you create then never look at again.

4.) **Do IT!** - and do it again, and again, and again, and again. Keep doing it. Over and over again. And do it some more. It is the doing it repeatedly over time which will change things. It will change the old patterns and behaviors into new patterns and behaviors. This is a lifestyle change. This is the **KEY COMPONENT** to creating wealth! When you fall off the wagon (just like on a diet), don't beat yourself up over it, just get back on the budget wagon. No big deal. This works over time, and if 90% of the time you are on budget, 10% of the time not on budget is no big deal.

5.) **Yearly Check-Up** - Just like good health needs a yearly check up, so does good wealth. Every year re-evaluate your goals, re-evaluate your spending and saving habits and re-assess your budget plan. Your personal finance will run like a well-oiled machine, and after time you will see that it is just like running your own business.

Only YOU own the printing press on this money machine!

2 BUDGET

Let's face it, doing a budget is never fun, and nothing in life ever goes as planned. That goes double and triple for money matters. How many times has it happened that you have finally worked and worked and worked and you have a little breathing room in your budget, then an unexpected expense comes along (like a flat tire, or a broken tooth) and wipes it out.

One way to prepare for the unexpected is to do a budget. Unfortunately, the word 'budget' sounds a lot like the word 'diet' to me, and I HATE/LOATHE/HATE diets. The connotation of 'budget' makes me think of 'can't have', 'lack', 'not enough'. So I say let's change the word budget to 'Spending Plan!' that sounds more fun. Almost like calling a diet a 'Dessert Plan' instead. See how that just makes you feel better?

A 'Spending Plan' is the difference between the rich and the not-so-rich.

So grab a pen!

Step One: Establishing Your Goals

Since you have already done an evaluation and assessment on yourself, let's roll up our sleeves and get to the fun part. GOALS!

Short Term Goals:

Short term goals are things you would like to achieve within the first 3 years of creating your new 'Spending Plan'. This is fun.

What are your short term goals? Are they:
The purchase of a new car?
A vacation?
Buying a new home theater sound system?

It doesn't matter what it is, just make sure it is something you want! These short term goals can also be used as markers and rewards for keeping you on track in your 'Spending Plan'

Brainstorm NOW!

Intermediate Goals:

These are goals that you would like to achieve within the next ten years. This could be:
To start a new career,
Start your own business,
Send your child to private school or college or
Even save up for a house down-payment.

This will take a little bit of time, a little bit of planning, but more important, this is the where your financial health is going to be in the not so distant future.

Take your time, and make it a good one!

Long Term Goals:

This is the part where you can shoot for the moon.
Do you want to retire by 65?
Do you want to buy a vacation home?
Would you like to leave a financial legacy to your heirs?

This is the Coup d'etat of your 'Spending Plan', the masterpiece, the final curtain call. This is what all the awesome planning and saving and spending has led you to.

This one might be a little more difficult to think of, especially in these uncertain economic times, but don't let it stop you from dreaming. If your goal is to have $5 million in the bank by the time you are 65, it will have nothing to do with wether or not you get a social security check. What I want you to focus on, are your own personal goals and what you want!

Do you have your goals written down?

Great! Let's move on.

3 ESTIMATE YOUR INCOME

Do you get a paycheck? Tips? Child support? Alimony? Unemployment? Did you inherit money that comes in the mail every week? Do you have a sugar mama/daddy?

AWESOME!

Whatever it is, getting money is awesome. Take a moment and write it down – (in the chart included) - then add up all the income sources you have. Include any take-home pay, interest, dividends, etc. Do not include 'projected raises', overtime pay or bonus'. If your income fluctuates, UNDERESTIMATE your income for this spending plan's purpose, this includes tips! You will thank me later. Promise.

Then - minus away all the taxes.

Category	Budget	Actual	Difference
Wages			
Interest			
Investments			
Misc.			
Income Subtotal			
Federal Tax			
State/Local Tax			
Social Security Tax			
Income Tax Total			
Spendable Income!			

4 ESTIMATE YOUR EXPENSES

I have attached a handy chart. I have added all sorts of categories, so just skip it if it doesn't apply to you. If I have forgotten something, just add it to the bottom. This is not a static worksheet and will change each month as your spending changes. But this will give you a good starting point on perhaps where the pennies are leaking out of your life.

You might need a few drafts of this.

Category	Budget Amount	Actual Amount	Difference
Mortgage/ Rent			
Homeowner /Renters Ins.			
Property Taxes			
Home repairs			
Electricity			
Water/Sewer			
Natural Gas/Oil			
Telephone/ Cell			
Groceries			

Eating out/lunch/ snack/coffee			
Child Support			
Day Care			
Insurance			
Out of pocket medical expenses			
Fitness (yoga, gym, massage)			
Car payment			
Gas/Oil/ Repairs			
Auto			

Insurance			
Other (tolls, bus fare, subway, taxi)			
Debit Payments**			
Credit Card			
Student Loan			
Other / Personal Loans			

**DEBIT PAYMENTS - consolidate your debit payments here for the ease of this worksheet. If you do not have a credit card, CONGRATULATIONS! If you do, and have more than one with multiple balances - use the next worksheet before going any further.

Credit Card break-down budget sheet

Credit Card	Lender	Amount Owed	Min. Monthly Payment	Rate
Sample	*Name of bank*	*$3,000.00*	*$120.00*	*19.00%*

*Put your subtotal in the 'Credit Card' box on the previous worksheet.

All of these steps are critical for getting you organized.

Now on to the fun part:

Category	Budget	Actual	Difference
Entertainment Recreation			
Cable TV / Movies/Videos			
Computer			
Hobbies			
Subscriptions / Dues			
Vacation			

If you want a vacation - you have to have a 'Spending Plan' for it!

Category	Budget	Actual	Difference
Pets – Food / Grooming			
Clothing			
Investment / Savings			
401(k)/IRA			
Stocks/ Bonds			
College Fund			
Savings			
Emergency $			
Household			
Gifts			

Category	Budget	Actual	Difference
Donations			
Hair/ Make-up			
Other expense			
Total			

Add it all up!

*For expenses incurred more or less monthly, convert the payment to a monthly amount when calculating the monthly budget.

5 BALANCE YOUR SPENDING PLAN!

This is easy - but might take a few tries.
Subtract fixed expenses from your expected income.

Then, subtract the total amount of flexible expenses from what is left of income.

If you need to cut back on your expenses, start first with the flexible expenses, then move to irregular expenses, and finally, to fixed expenses.

If you have a surplus after subtracting expenses from income, GREAT JOB! By not skimping on your savings, put your extra income to paying off your credit card debt. If you do not have any credit card debt, put it towards your savings, investment portfolio or other Mid and Long Term Goals!

6 ADJUST YOUR BUDGET

Adjust budget plan figures if necessary, based on the record keeping in Chapter 5. It may take several months of adjusting and re-adjusting before your plan works smoothly. The real payoff of working with a budget plan and keeping records will come when you use your past year's budget and records to plan for the future. Budget records can help you pinpoint spending leaks or spot potential trouble before it occurs.

GREAT JOB!

The hard part is over.

Now on to the tips and tricks from the trade to make it easy.

Smart Budgeting

Everyone has their own way of keeping track of their finances. No one is right or wrong, they just have their own way of doing things. Here are a few tricks or tips that might be helpful for you. But remember, this is your budget! Set it up how YOU want it. You are the one who is going to have to live with it.

Ideas that might help:

*Keep it simple. Don't detail your plan to the penny. Keep track to the nearest dollar or even the nearest five dollars. This works only if you set your "breaking point" and stick to it. For example, if you prefer to keep track to the nearest dollar, set $.50 as your breaking point. If the amount to be recorded is $49.49, you drop the cents and write down $49. But if the amount is $49.50, you write $50. Such a system keeps some of the drudgery out of record keeping.

*Be realistic. Consider all expenses, including vacations, spending money, alcohol, tobacco and hobbies. To build in a margin of safety in your plan, overestimate your expenses and underestimate your income. *VERY IMPORTANT*

*Don't expect someone else's budget to work for you. When you see a budget in the newspaper or magazine, realize it is for a particular situation or for an "average" or "typical" family. It's important to tailor a spending plan to your individual needs and situation. Distinguish between wants and needs. Buy what you need first. The wants belong in the "what's left over" category.

Borrow with care. Remember, you create a fixed expense each time you charge something or pay "on time." Even though it might give you pleasure to own something right now, consider all the interest you'll be paying and ask yourself if it's really worth the price. If possible, use cash for ALL your impulse purchases. We will go into more detail of this in a minute.

*Plan for and develop an emergency fund! This is perhaps the most important element of all.

*Everyone will have a different method - I know a man who budgets and swears by the envelope method - taking all of his money for the month out in cash and distributing it into envelopes, and once it is gone... it's gone.

Speaking of Cash...
CASH IS KING!

More and more I find people going all cash, or getting rid of their credit cards. There are many reasons I have heard of people doing this, including:

*I'll spend less. - A variety of scientific studies, such as one at the Massachusetts Institute of Technology, have found that people are simply willing to spend more when they use credit cards than they do when they use cash. It's common sense. No wonder our national obsession with shopping really took off when credit cards came on the scene.

*The card bonuses really aren't worth it. - A lot of people use their credit cards for the frequent flyer miles or other bonuses. But many of these deals are getting less valuable. Some people who do this can get up to 2% back on their cards. Compared to the extra amount of time, effort and energy you spend to track and pay, that's chicken feed.

*Cash makes budgeting easy. - Like I said before, I have a friend who pulls out all the cash he needs for his budget, separates it all out into envelopes, and when it is gone, it's GONE.

Less worry about identity theft. - 'Nuff said.

Fewer impulse purchases. - Stores are capitalistic and opportunistic. There is a very scientific method and sophisticated marketing science to manipulate you into reaching into your wallet. If you don't have the money on you, you can't 'splurge'. If you really want the item, you can come back any buy it tomorrow, but chances are... you wont.

Shopping online is still easy - Go to your local bank and buy a prepaid card to charge up with cash. This works great when you are traveling and making airline and hotel reservations.

Say goodbye to debt. - I pay my cards off in full every month, but a lot of people don't. They use their cards to borrow, and it's a financial disaster. We've seen what the overuse of debt has done to our economy. Some easy calculations will show you that if you buy something for $1,000 on your credit card which charges 14% interest, and you pay the minimum balance each month, it will take you 110 months to pay off the bill, AND at the end of the 110 months, you have just spent $1750 on a $1000 item. It is just silly.

*Privacy. Credit cards are great for tracking people. They tell you exactly what you bought, where and when. Personally, I love the privacy and anonymity of cash.

*Cash supports the local economy - The money I spend locally goes to the merchant and his suppliers. When I go into my local credit union to cash a check, I'm keeping a couple of local tellers in work.

Credit Cards - Oh how I loathe thee...

I am putting the average American Credit Card user on notice - > If you have to put something on a credit card - you can't afford it. When it comes down to it, if you're putting the new stove or sofa on a credit card (or even worse, a store credit card) then you really shouldn't be buying that item at all. Remember, back in the day people used to do this crazy thing called "saving." Today, we're all about instant gratification. Buy now, pay later. And by the time we're finished paying something off, it's time to get a new one. The cycle never ends.

It is time to "Stop the Spending Insanity!"

Remember that $1000 item? Did you really need to have it? Doesn't matter any more, today is the day you can stop overspending, take back your finances and build your wealth!

How do you know which card to pay off first?

I am glad you asked! Do you remember at the 'tracking expenses part' we filled out a credit card worksheet. You are going to need that again.

Take a look at that sheet, and using those numbers, you can easily fill in the following. This will give you an accurate idea of how long it will take to pay off each of your cards, AND which one will be paid off first assuming you continue to make the minimum payments.

Account	Balance	Min. Monthly Payment	Balance divided by Min. Monthly Payment	Rank Lowest to Highest
Sample	$3,000.00	$120.00	25	1
Sample #2	$6,700.00	$215.00	31	2

Once you have paid off one credit card, add the minimum monthly payment to the next card to pay off.

DO NOT JUST KEEP THE EXTRA MONEY TO SPEND ON OTHER THINGS!

This goes without saying - Your credit card should be locked away. We have already done the 'spending plan' and balanced your budget. There is no need for you to be spending beyond your means anymore and digging a bigger hole.

This is the part that separates the 'men from the boys'. The goal is to NOT give other people your money for free. Paying interest is nothing more than giving away your money.

But why do you overspend in the first place?
Just STOP!

Simplify!

You will never be able to fill an emotional void in your life by buying more stuff. You will never be better or different if you own those shoes or that pair of pants. Stores are designed to make you WANT THINGS. That is their job. Your job is to be strong in your willpower and not succumb to the 'consumer whore' attitude that is the American culture.

America is a capitalistic economy, if we don't spend, the economy slows. Yet we as Americans are trillions of dollars in debt from overspending. We have, for years, effectively trained ourselves, like Pavlov's dogs, to shop.

You have the power to STOP. If you feel as though you can't stop, seek help! Don't carry your credit cards in your wallet or purse, pay with cash (only), tell your friends what you are doing so they can support you and remind you when you fall off the wagon, don't go to an ATM more than once a week, barter for goods and services by using your talents and gifts, host a 'naked lady party' or swap party where you and your friends can exchange goods like shoes, clothes, handbags and household items and if you still can't stop spending, seek help.

Professional help.

There are many credit and financial counselors available.

If you really want to get serious about stopping unnecessary spending, I throw down the gauntlet...
with

THE PENNY CHALLENGE!

The Penny Challenge:

TRACK EVERY PENNY YOU SPEND IN ONE
DAY
This nice chart will put it in black and white if
what you just bought was really worth it.

What you bought	How much did you spend?	Was it worth it?
Latte	*$3.45*	*No*

My Latte was $3.45

If I bought one latte every day ($3.45 x 30) =
$103.50

One latte a day for a year ($3.45 x 365) =
$1,259.25

One latte a day for 10 years ($3.45 x 3650) =
$12,592.50

If I invested my 'latte':

In 10 years it would be worth = $12,592.50
In 20 years it would be worth = $25,185.00
In 30 years it would be worth = $37,777.50
In 40 years it would be worth = $50,370.00

This doesn't even take into consideration the 8th wonder of the world called **COMPOUNDING INTEREST**. Compounding interest is usually the nasty thing that credit card companies do when you have a balance with them (by adding interest to the principle, so not only are you paying on the original interest, but also interest on the original interest) Only this time, imagine that **YOU** are the credit card company and you are making the compounding interest on the Latte that they bought.

**It is GENIUS!   MAGIC!
And SO EASY!**

After 10 years at an interest rate of just 4%, your $3.45 daily investment would be worth:
$17,587.44

After 10 years and the cost of a coffee, you just made $4,994.94 of FREE MONEY and now have $20,000 in your pocket!

WHAT IF????

What if you've gone through the first five steps and you can' t free up enough money to start repaying your debts in a big way?

Then you have three choices.

You can consider whether the big-ticket items in your life—your home, your cars, private schools—are truly necessary.

2.   You can go through your home and your possessions and see if there's anything value to sell.

3.   You can earn more money, either on your current job or—more likely—by taking on a second one.

The other alternatives? Credit counseling and bankruptcy—but you're not there yet. For now, let's see what you can accomplish on your own.

Here are some other options you may want to consider.

<u>Moving.</u>

Is your housing sabotaging your ability to make ends meet? It is for a lot of people. During the last decade or so, we were so afraid that if we didn't buy right now we'd be priced out of the only neighborhood we wanted to live in. It may be that selling your house is a solution you have to consider. Yes, the conventional wisdom is that your house is the asset you'll retire on (and often retire in)—the most valuable asset in your portfolio. But unless you can afford to make the payments, it's also the one that can be your Achilles heel. Perhaps you can trade down—swapping a larger house for something more manageable and less expensive. You also may need to consider renting for a while. As long as you can keep the cost of moving reasonable (recruit your friends), renting will save you the cost of homeowner's insurance. (You'll need renters insurance, but it's much cheaper.) You'll save on yard care and—depending on where you relocate—may be able to cut your commuting costs as well.

<u>Going carless.</u>

There probably is—if you dig down deep and consider it—another, less-expensive way for you to get back and forth to work each day. Could you get by without a car for a while? That wouldn't only save you the cost of paying for the car itself and it's upkeep, but for gasoline, auto insurance, parking. And if you can't go carless, how about trading in your pricey car for one that runs just fine but is used and less luxurious.

<u>Sell your stuff</u>

When big corporations are looking to lower debt and boost profits, one of their primary strategies is to sell assets. They sell divisions, product lines, inventory, equipment. You can do the same on a smaller scale. What possessions do you have that might be valuable on the open market? Which could you part with if it meant financial security? Your boat? Second car? Second home? Time share? Art or jewelry? To get the most for whatever you're selling, you need to know what it's worth. If it's truly valuable (think $5,000 or more) you should have it appraised for your sake and for tax purposes. If it's a household item that's not worth having appraised, you can get an accurate idea of fair market value by seeing what similar items are selling for through classified advertisements (like Craigslist) or on eBay.

If you find you have nothing big of value but lots of little things to sell, there's a solution as American as apple pie...

Have a great garage sale.
Don't just throw your junk in a pile and expect it to fly out of your garage or your yard. Approach it methodically and you'll clean up financially—and clean up your garage. Pick a date at least a few weeks out. Saturdays are best. Then, go through your house and decide what goes. If you haven't used an item in two years, you can live without it.

Next, organize the merchandise—putting like with like—so buyers can find what they're looking for. If you're selling clothing, put it on a rack or string up a clothesline and hang it for people to see. If you're not sure you have enough to fill your yard, collaborate with a few families. In order to keep track of who's earned what, put different color price tags on each family's items. Then make sure whoever's minding the register knows the code.

Don't forget to advertise by running ads in local papers and on the Internet (there are lots of free yard and garage sale sites).

Ask for a raise.

We know you work hard already, but sometimes the only way to dig out is by earning extra money. You may be able to do that at your own job. If it's been a year or more since you received a raise, it's time to ask for one. If you don't get it, ask your supervisor what you need to do to increase the size of your paycheck.

Moonlight.

You may need to get a second job. Eight and a half million Americans have already done so to meet regular household expenses or pay off debt, according to the Bureau of Labor Statistics. That's 4 out of 10 people! If you're already moonlighting and it's been a while since you raised your rates or raised your prices, do so today by 10%. That's the easiest way to pad your pocket.

Without managing your expenses, your wants and needs will invariably outpace your ability to earn. By implementing some form of budgeting, you can begin to set your sights on saving and meeting your longer-term financial objectives.

7 LONG TERM PLANNING

Once you've accumulated sufficient funds to cover your emergency needs and purchased protection against financial risks, you can begin saving for your long-term goals in earnest. This is also the part where you should be thinking about establishing a relationship with a licensed Financial Advisor.

Good Financial Advisors advertise, GREAT Financial Advisors don't have to.
<u>Why?</u>

Great Financial Advisors usually have clients who will tout their capability and skill, and just by word of mouth, they find great clients.

WORD OF MOUTH.

That means - Ask around.

Set up an interview with a prospective agent and ask questions.

Ask to see their credentials.
Ask how long they have been in business.
Ask for references.
Ask about their specific niche.
Ask about their investment philosophy.
Ask them about their book of business.
Look for a fiduciary (which means they have pledged to act in the client's best interest - similar to the Hippocratic oath, only for investors).
Ask what their background is.
Ask how they get paid.

All Financial Advisors worth their weight will be up front and honest. Here are some topics of conversation to have on hand once you have found someone you are comfortable with and are ready to take the next step of amassing and growing your wealth.

Ample Insurance Protection
A major disability, the loss of a family breadwinner, a fire in your home, a family member's major medical problem or need for skilled nursing care ... the most dramatic emergencies can seldom be paid for completely using personal savings.

Although such tragedies can create devastating individual financial hardship, the financial risk of such events can be shared by very large groups of families and individuals through insurance. Life insurance, disability income insurance, property and casualty (P&C) insurance, long-term-care insurance, and major medical insurance all have a place in your "Life Cycle Planning."

Ensuring Adequate Liquidity

As your budget begins to pay off in a healthy savings account, you might begin to wonder how best to apply your limited savings to your unlimited needs and wants. Without exception, the first financial need you should meet is to have an emergency fund. An emergency fund allows us to cover unexpected short-term needs using cash instead of leveraging your future earnings through costly loans. As a general rule of thumb, your emergency fund should be adequate to maintain your standard of living for six months.

Turn Protection into Profit

As you start to pay down your debts, siphon off a chunk of money each month—3–5% is a good start but aim for 10%—and put it into savings. Stash your savings in a safe place, such as the highest paying money market account you can find until you've got a substantial emergency cushion equivalent to 3 to 6 months salary. That's your protection. If you get laid off, if the dog gets ill, if your transmission dies, you'll be able to live and pay your bills without sliding back. Once you've got your emergency cushion, you can start investing that money in a portfolio of stocks and mutual funds that can help you build a real foundation of wealth for your future.

Life Cycle Planning

Financial planning means something different to everyone. For some, it's about getting by month to month on their paycheck, for others it's about watching how their stock portfolio performs each day. Unfortunately, few of us feel completely prepared to meet our ongoing financial obligations and objectives.

Worries about money have become one of the greatest anxieties of our day - witness the dramatic rise in financial-related publications, radio and television shows, and websites.Because each person's situation, lifestyle, and goals are so different, there is no single turnkey solution for successful money management. However, a great financial advisor can identify several steps that successful people take in pursuing their financial goals.

8 THE VALUE OF TIME

Human capital refers a person's ability to turn their skills and abilities into a livelihood. The development of these skills and abilities helps us maximize our income potential in a competitive marketplace. In our early working years, usually between age 18 and 25, we set ourselves on a course that largely defines our human capital potential. Each of us makes an investment in human capital, whether we realize it or not. For some this is an investment of time, gaining experience and skills on the job. For others it is an investment in trade school or college. It should also be noted that, although our greatest focus on human capital development generally takes place in our early years, this is an investment we should continue to make and assess throughout our working careers. Your ability to earn income, now and in the future, is the most valuable asset you own.

Many people often overlook the time value of money. Economists know full well that a dollar received today is worth more than a dollar received a year from now. Why? Because that dollar could be invested, saved, or used to purchase an asset such as real estate that will appreciate in value. What's more, inflation slowly but steadily erodes the purchasing power of your money, rendering tomorrow's dollar less valuable than today's.

The relationship between time and money provides the foundation for virtually every financial decision you will make. Whether you are saving money for a future event or considering a loan to pay for a current financial need, you will be greatly affected by the time value of money. The following are some tips for making the most of your dollars, today and tomorrow.

Whether you are saving for retirement or a down payment on a home, college funding or dependent care needs, you will be greatly affected by these simple time value tips.

Time Value Tip #1: The longer you have to prepare, the less your objectives will cost. Assuming you are able to invest your savings and earn a positive return, you will always be better off saving for your goals in advance. Not only will your savings earn interest, but the interest you earn will also begin to earn interest. COMPOUNDING INTEREST - remember - It was referred to by Albert Einstein as the "the most powerful force in the universe." (No one knows whether he was serious or joking.) Credit card companies have figured this out, it is about time that you put it to your own benefit!

Time Value Tip #2: The higher the rate of return you are able to secure on your savings, the faster your money will grow. Generally, the amount of risk you are willing to take on your investments will determine your long-term rate of return. The longer you have to save for your goals, the more risk you should take on your investments, and the greater rate of return you should expect.

Time Value Tip #3: It's almost always better to postpone paying taxes on your investment proceeds. When you have the choice, you should usually choose to delay paying taxes on investment proceeds as long as possible. That's because as long as you retain all your investment's growth, instead of losing some to taxes, you can continue to earn more interest on that growth. Once you pay the taxes, you will never earn interest on those lost funds again. One way to postpone the payment of taxes is to invest in qualified retirement plans, such as IRAs and 401(k) accounts. Another tactic is to invest in annuities, which also allow your money to grow tax-free until withdrawn.

Time Value Tip #4: Factor inflation into your long-term plans. When preparing for long-term financial objectives, you must factor inflation into your plan. Over the last 20 years, inflation has averaged about 4% per year. At that rate, in 20 years a salary of $50,000 will buy what only $22,100 does in today's dollars - that's less than half. Looked at another way, that $30,000 luxury car you've had your eye on will cost you a whopping $67,872 just two decades from now! The cost of some financial objectives will grow even faster than this -- college costs, for example, have increased by some 8% annually on average. Planning for such cost increases will ensure that your asset accumulation level is sufficient to meet your objectives.

What's the best time to start preparing for a sound financial future?

Twenty years ago, goes the old joke.

Failing that, the second-best time is today.

ABOUT THE AUTHOR

Armed with a MBA, Rae spent 14 long years in corporate America. From stocks to bonds, insurance to investments, mergers to acquisitions. She lived in the inside of the money machine and has great knowledge of how to make more out of what you have. In 2004 Rae started doing private business consulting and stress management seminars and was a featured speaker at many continuing education gatherings and internationally recognized colleges.